ANGER MANAGEMENT SKILLS FOR CHILDREN

ELEMENTARY

IDA GREENE, Ph.D.

ISBN 1-881165-08-6

ATTENTION COLLEGES AND UNIVERSITIES, CORPORATIONS, AND PROFESSIONAL ORGANIZATIONS: Quantity discounts are available on bulk purchases of this book for educational training purposes, fund raising, or gift giving. For information contact: **P. S. I. Publishers, 2910 Baily Ave. San Diego, CA 92105 (619) 262-9951.**

FOREWORD

We are feeling, caring, and loving people, and that is good. The problem is that we sometimes we overreact, react at the wrong time, or react in a way that make others feel sad, hurt or feel you do not care about their feelings.

I hope this workbook will help you improve the way you talk and behave, so that everyone including you feel happy. When you speak softly and slowly others can hear what you say and respond to you in a calm tone of voice. Your tone of voice, the rate at which you speak, the way you sit or stand, the smile or frown on your face, looking in the eyes of a person or looking away from a person sends a message about you to the other person. Communication is everything you think, say or do. If what you say and do is done in a pleasant manner, others are less likely to see as an angry person.

All emotions are good. Your actions, the words you use, and the tone of voice you use will make others like or dislike you. The way you speak to others, and the way treat them, will let them know how much you care about their feelings. What you say, the way in which you speak, and your friendliness will tell others how feel about you and them and will respond to you.

ACKNOWLEDGEMENTS

I give thanks to both the good and unpleasant encounters I have experienced. I give thanks for the pleasant and unpleasant people I have met, I have learned from both. Some life lessons can be taught and other lessons have to be brought through pain and hardship.

Hopefully you will be a student of life and learn from other mistakes.

I wish to thank Catherine Bozigian for creating the charts in this book

Ida Greene, Ph.D.

Anger Management Skills
for the
Elementary School Child

This book is geared toward the younger child and his or her parents. The worksheets help the child release their feelings about anger without making it boring. The worksheets will also allow the parent to view the child's real sources of anger.

Reading This Book Can Help You If:
1. You are misunderstood, most of the time
2. You fear being misunderstood
3. Have poor interpersonal skills
4. Have problems with Anxiety or Fear
5. Disagreement or conflict between you and others
6. Have self-limitations or overly shy
7. Lack of self boundaries, or others make "fun" of you
8. Inability to say "No" or cannot accept "No"
9. Have trouble coping with rejection
10. Strong willed, or Inflexible
11. Low frustration, Impatient or easily get upset about things
12. Blame others for all your problems.
13. Feel you are perfect, and do not need to change or improve
14. You have to be "Right" all the Time.
15. You are demanding, feel others have to listen to you
16. Other people are afraid of you
17. You are a Bully and threaten others
18. You insist on getting your way.

THE BENEFITS OF ANGER MANAGEMENT

1. Reduce the number of times and seriousness of behavior that cause others to avoid playing with you or being friends with you.

2. Decrease and eliminate annoying behaviors toward family members and friends.

3. Express your feelings in a kind and respectful manner.

4. Notice how what you say and the tone of voice you use affect your friends, playmates and family members.

5. Help you notice how the expression on your face, like a frown make others feel about you.

Anger Management Skills
for the Elementary Schoolchild

One thing that any child can do to enhance their self-esteem is to be in control of all negative emotions. A negative emotion is any emotion that can cause harm to another person, create friction between you and another person, or be a source of conflict, cause damage to a relationship, or to destroy frienship between you and another child.

Anger can be like a sword when it is not controlled. The following are emotions I consider harmful or hurtful : Envy, Jealousy, Getting even with some one, Name calling, Fear, Hate, and Anger. All of these feelings are addressed extensively in the book, *Light the Fire Within You*. Anger will be discussed here because it is often the cause of problems between you and other class mates.

Anger is a powerful emotion, so you will have to decide if you will express it or keep it inside. You alone decide if you will get angry, pout or hit someone when you are upset about something. You decide how you will react to what someone says to you. Your tolerance for emotional pain will be the deciding factor. Anger is a signal for you, to look at what is going on in your body to see what is causing you to feel upset, frustrated or confused.

Often when we are angry, one or more of these things are going on:
1. We want something and are not getting it.
2. We are afraid someone will say "No" to us.
3. We believe getting our way is a sign of love.

The goal of anger management is for you to use your anger (negative feelings) as a way to identify your problem/s and solve it, rather than act upon your frustrations by lashing out or holding your angry feelings inside.

YOUR SELF-CONCEPT/SELF-IDENTITY IS COMPOSED OF:
A *thought* is an unspoken word
A *word* is a spoken thought
Behavior is *a thought and a word*

TRUST ME!

ANSWER THE QUESTIONS BELOW:

Five people I trust are

- ....

- ....

- ....

- ....

- ....

I trust them because ....

....

....

....

I think ....*(number)* **people trust me.**

They trust me because ....

....

....

....

I can earn other people's trust by ....

....

....

....

MY PERFECT FAMILY

If you could change your family, what would it look like? Draw yourself at the larger circle, and the rest of your ideal family in the other circles. Then on the lines below, write why you would like each person to be in your family.

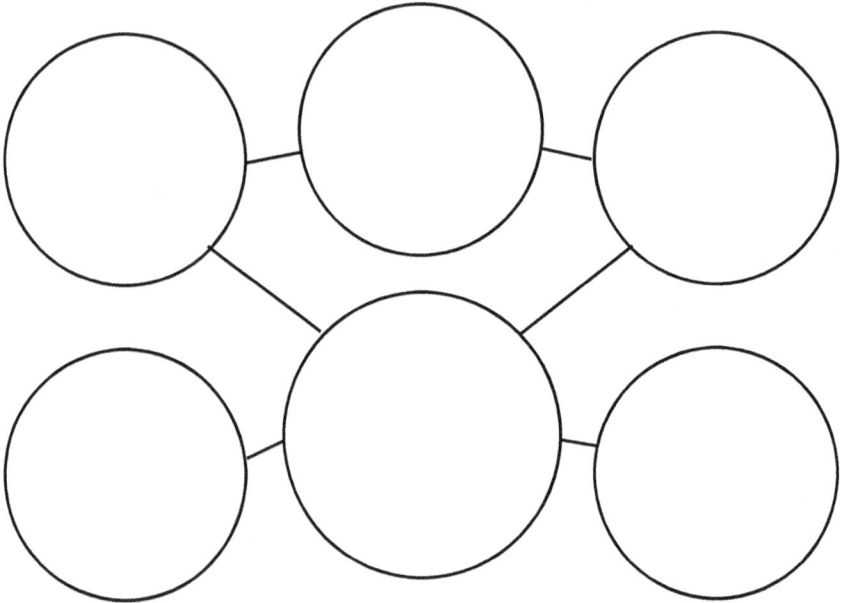

My Real Family

In the spaces below, write the the names of five members of your family. Across from their name, tell what you like to do with that person.

FAMILY MEMBER
Example: Mom

WHAT I LIKE TO DO WITH THEM
Example: Play games, dance

1. _____

1. _____

   _____

2. _____

2. _____

   _____

3. _____

3. _____

   _____

4. _____

4. _____

   _____

5. _____

5. _____

   _____

If I Could Change My Appearance

Some people aren't happy with the way they look and want to change a few things about themselves. Maybe you don't like the way your body looks or the size of your feet. Draw what you look like now in one box and in the other; draw what you want to look like.

ME NOW

HOW I WANT TO BE

You Can Count On Me!

We all count upon others for certain things. How do you count on these people and what do they count on you for? Complete the blanks below.

I count on Mom or Dad for	I count on my teacher for
_____ _____	_____ .
My Mom or Dad counts on me to	My teacher counts on me to
_____ _____	_____ _____
I count on my friend for	I count on my brother or sister for
_____ _____	_____ _____
My friend counts on me for	He or she counts on me to
_____ _____	_____ _____

Story Time

Write a short story including all of the characters below. Talk about what they do together, if they get along, and what they might fight about.

Dr. Blue   **Mr. Smiles**   **Miss Grumpy**   **Sir Yells a Lot**

Example: Mr. Smiles doesn't like to play with Miss Grumpy a lot because she isn't as happy as he is.

....

....

....

....

....

....

....

....

....

....

....

....

....

WHAT I WANTED

Everyone has wanted something special. Maybe you wanted a dog or a new game. Sometimes, when we don't get these things, we feel bad. Answer the questions below about what you felt like when you didn't get what you wanted.

The special thing I wanted was:	I wanted it because:.............. ....
What did you want it for (Birthday, holidays, etc.)	Who did you want to do it? ....
Why didn't you get it?	Were you mad? ....

The next time I don't get what I want, instead of feeling mad, I'm going to:

....

....

....

....

DRAW IT!

Choose two people you know – they could be family members, friends or even teachers. Draw one picture of what they look like when they're happy and another of when they're mad. Then circle which picture of each person that you like better.

Happy   Mad

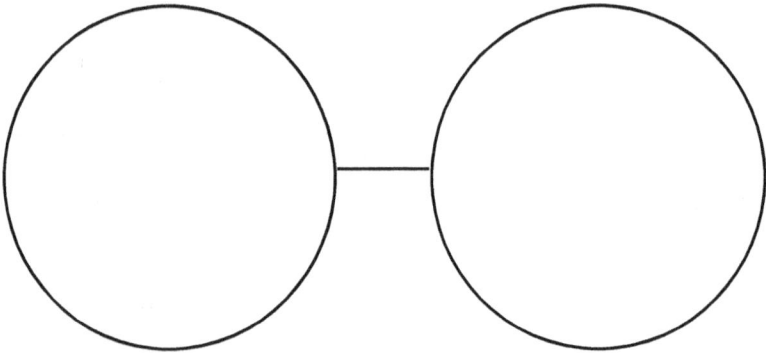

Happy   Mad

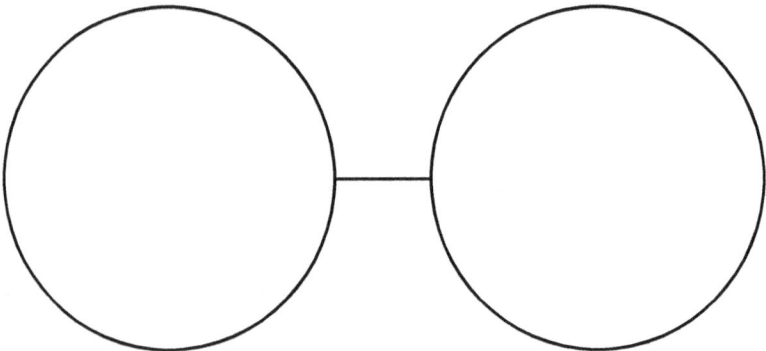

DRAW YOUR MOODS

The way you feel inside changes the way you look on the outside. When you're happy, you smile, and when you're upset, you frown. Draw in the circles below what you look like when you're upset and happy.

UPSET/ANGRY/SAD   **HAPPY**

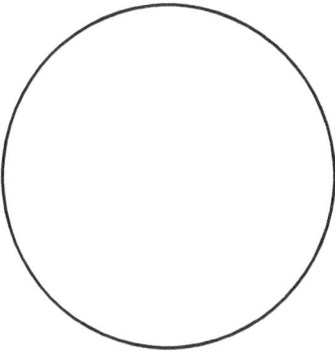
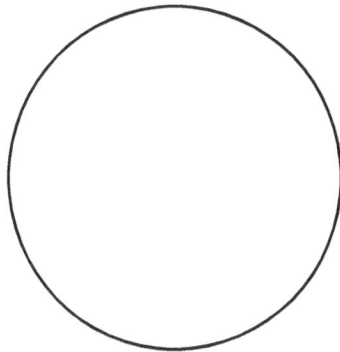

HOUSE RULES

Answer the questions below.

1. What objects in your house are you not allowed to touch?

....

....

2. What happens if you touch something you're not allowed?

....

....

....

3. What things are you "not allowed" to do, by yourself?

_ ....

....

....

4. What things are you "allowed" to do, by yourself?

....

....

....

5. Why do you think parents make these rules?

a. ....

b. ....

My Duties

In the spaces below list four duties you have at school and at home. Use the numbers below to indicate how dependable you are in doing your duties.

1 = poor; 2 = fair; 3 = good; 4 = excellent

School Duties	**Rating**
1.	....
2.	....
3.	....
4.	....
....	....

Home Duties	**Rating**
1.	....
2.	....
3.	....
4.	....

LOOK OUT! HERE I COME!

Check those things you do to get attention. Circle the one thing you do most often to get attention.

- ☐ Do dumb things
- ☐ Act sick
- ☐ Do things extra well so people will notice
- ☐ Don't talk
- ☐ Pout
- ☐ Pick on someone
- ☐ Pretend I am bored
- ☐ Cry
- ☐ Put others down
- ☐ Other_____

Ask your teacher to help you devise a plan for getting attention in more positive ways than those listed above. Describe your plan below.

_____

_____

_____

_____

_____

_____

NECESSARY RULES
Answer the questions below.

1. What would your house be like if you didn't have rules?

   ....

   ....

   ....

2. What would school be like if we didn't have rules?

   ....

   ....

   ....

3. If you were the teacher, what rules would you make for the class? List the 3 most important rules.

   a. ....

   b. ....

   c. ....

4. Would you make rules against hurting people's feelings? What would be some good rules?

   ....

   ....

   ....

5. What would be the punishment for breaking the rules?

   ....

   ....

   ....

THE CLASSROOM

Answer the questions below:

1. In which ways is the classroom like a family?

   ....

   ....

   ....

2. What type of members of the family is there? Who is the parent?

   ....

   ....

   ....

3. List how a school is like a society.

   ....

   ....

   ....

4. If you were the ruler of the class, would it be very controlled (dictatorship), democracy, (freedom to express oneself), or a monarchy (King or President)?

   ....

   ....

   ....

   ....

WHAT MAKES ME MAD

Answer the questions below:

Five people I get mad at are

_____,

_____,

_____,

_____ and

_____

I get mad at them because ....

....

....

....

I think people get mad at me in the same way.

They get mad at me because ....

....

....

....

I can stop making people mad by ....

....

....

....

A GLANCE INTO THE FUTURE

Complete the sentences below.

1. I want to become ....
   ....

2. When I graduate from college I would like to ....
   ....
   ....

3. When I'm an adult, I think I would like to ....
   ....
   ....

4. To be what I want to be when I'm an adult, I'll need to
   learn about ....
   ....

5. If I could change myself, I'd like to be more.....................
   ....
   and less ....
   ....

6. If I could move to anywhere in the world, it would be to
   ....

7. I would like to take these things or people with me when
   I move ....
   ....
   ....

REAL ME – POST TEST ASSESSMENT

Circle the word(s) or number(s) that best fit you.

1. I would describe myself as a *nice | smart | angry | happy* person.

2. Others would describe me as a *nice | smart | angry | happy* person.

3. I get angry *1-5 | 5-10 | 10-20* times a day.

4. When I'm angry I *cry | scream | don't talk*.

5. This person makes me angry a lot *mom/dad | brother/sister | friend | teacher*.

6. They make me angry because they don't *listen to me | let me do what I want | care about me*.

7. When I get mad, they *ignore me | get mad at me | make me feel better*.

8. When I'm angry, I feel *better | worse | the same* than when I'm happy.

9. What makes me feel better when I'm angry is *talking about why I'm angry | playing/singing/dancing | ignoring the problem*.

10. I *do | don't* like myself when I'm angry.

ANGER MANAGEMENT SELF EVALUATION

Name: ....Date:...........

Fill out this form each time you find yourself getting angry.

1. What was the situation? Who was present?

   ....

   ....

2. On a scale of 1 to 5, how angry were you? Write a number to show how you felt
   • Irritated
   • Embarrassed
   • Upset
   • Mad
   • Very Mad

3. What did you say or do to cause the problem?

   ....

   ....

4. Was your response necessary? ...... Was it inappropriate? ....
   Why?

   ....

   ....

5. What was the consequence of your response? Did you get what you wanted?...

Child (signature): ....

Parent/Guardian (signature) ....

MYSELF

I have to live with myself, and so
I want to be fit for myself to know,
I want to be able, as days go by,
Always to look myself straight in the eye;
I don't want to stand, with the setting sun,
And hate myself for the things I've done.
I don't want to keep on a closet shelf,
a lot of secrets about myself.
And fool myself, as I come and go,
Into thinking that nobody else will know
The kind of person that I really am;
I don't want to dress up myself in a sham.
I want to go out with my head erect,
I want to deserve all men's respect;
But here in the struggle for fame and self,
I want to be able to like myself.
I don't want to look at myself and know
That I'm bluster and bluff and empty show,
I never can hide myself from me;
I see what others may never see;
I know what others may never know;
I never can fool myself, and so,
Whatever happens, I want to be
Self-respecting and conscience free.

— EDGAR A. GUEST

What is an Anger Workout?

Remember, anger is a powerful emotion. It causes to think, act and behave in a way that can make others like or dislike us. When we are angry, we say hurtful things to others without thinking. The goal is for you to be in control of your temper on an hourly and daily basis. Taking a deep breath before you speak can help speak calmly. Be in control of your words, your actions, and your attitude. Learn to speak kind words in a kind tone of voice to others.

Just as our body needs an exercise workout, our emotions need a workout. An anger work-out is you noticing how others respond to you and the words you say to them. Pay attention to how others react to you often. We have to work through our frustrations and feelings about things that upset, continually.

When we care about the feelings of others, it makes us feel good about ourselves, the other person and the situation that caused you to become upset. We have to work on our feelings of anger just as we have to work out and exercise our body muscles. When you stop working on controlling your frustrations, it will show up as anger and it can hurt everyone including you. The more you work on controlling your anger, the less the chance for someone to be hurt by your temper outburst or bad mood.

Start today to take a deep breath before you speak and take two or three deeps breaths when you feel irritated, confused or upset with someone about something. Think and pause for a second or one minute before you say or do anything. This will help you to respond in a more loving way and others will feel better about you. Anger is neither, good or bad. It is just an emotion, when anger is used in the right way, others love to be around you and they want to be your friend.

***

Parents if you desire coaching for your child, or parenting classes, I can be reached at:

Tel.: 619-262-9951, or
www.selfesteemcenter.org, or
www.idagreene.com
E-mail: idagreene@idagreene.com

We have several books to assist the family, they are:
Anger Management Skills for Men
Anger Management Skills for Women
How to Improve Self-Esteem in Any Child
*How to Improve Self-Esteem in the
    African American Child*
 Self-Esteem the Essence of You
Light the Fire Within You
Soft Power Negotiation Skills
Money – How to Get It, How to Keep It
How to be a Success in Business
Are You Ready for Success?
*Say Goodbye to Your Smallness, Say Hello to
    Your Greatness*
    and
Stirring Up the African American Spirit.

Now You Keep Track of
When Someone Made You Mad
and How You Responded